Chips and a Splash

Written by Tony Dallas

Illustrated by Lhaiza Morena

This is Nana. She is Jamaican.

I am Moo Moo.

We were all going to the coast.
"I like the coast," said Nana.

Nana was a little sad.
"There are no crowds or soft sand!"
she said.

Come on,
Nana!

"Can we still have fun when there is no sun?" said Nana.

"Yes! We can splash!" I said.

Nana ran back out, yelling,
"It is freezing in there!"

We sat on deckchairs.
"What is that good smell?" Nana said.
"Food!" I said. "Shall we get some?"

"No!" said Nana.
"That gull took my chip!"

"Can I get a stick of rock?" I said, tugging Nana's arm.

Nana pointed at a rock.

"You can have this one!" she said.

"Rock is a sweet, Nana!" I said.

Nana bit the stick of rock.

"I do not like this coast," said Nana.
"I think you might like it out there!"
I said.

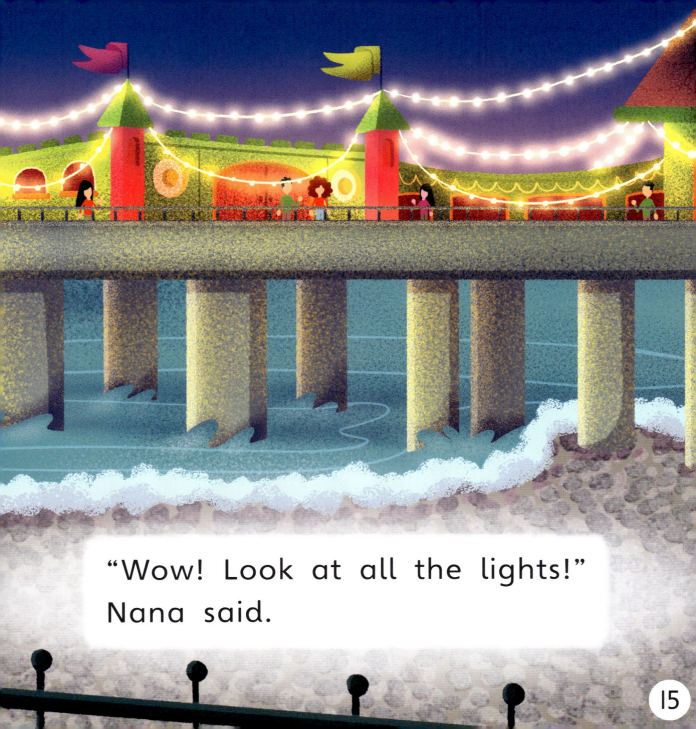

"Wow! Look at all the lights!"
Nana said.

"Do you like it?" I said.

"I do, Moo Moo!" Nana said.

"This is so much fun!"